LISTENING

NEW & SELECTED WORK

ALSO BY CHARLES ENTREKIN

Novel
Red Mountain; Birmingham, Alabama, 1965; 2008

Poetry
In This Hour; 1999
Casting for the Cutthroat & Other Poems; 1986
Casting for the Cutthroat; 1978
All Pieces of a Legacy; 1975

LISTENING

NEW & SELECTED WORK

CHARLES ENTREKIN

POETIC MATRIX PRESS

Poetic Matrix Press
P.O. Box 1223
Madera, CA 93639
www.poeticmatrix.com

DEDICATION

For Gail: generous spirit, playful wood sprite,
advocate, trusted companion, soul mate, wife.

ACKNOWLEDGMENTS

I would like to thank the following: The wonderfully talented
and generous readers who helped me make the difficult choices
concerning what to include in this anthology. They are:
Barbara Joan Tiger Bass, Catherine Anderson, Judy Crowe,
Karla Arens, Paul Dolinsky, Stewart Florsheim, and Gail Rudd
Entrekin. And I especially want to thank John Peterson and
Poetic Matrix Press for making this anthology possible.

CONTENTS

DEDICATION
ACKNOWLEDGEMENTS

FROM ALL PIECES OF A LEGACY (1975)

ALABAMA KUDZU / 3
ALL PIECES OF A LEGACY / 4
AWAKENING / 5
BALLAD / 6
LET'S PLAY A GAME / 7
BIRMINGHAM / 8
COUSIN DINK / 9
PARTING / 10
MISSOULA SPRING / 11
MONTANA / 12
ON YOUR BIRTHDAY / 13
IN SAN FRANCISCO / 14
HAMBURGERS / 15
THE PALACE OF NEW BEGINNINGS / 19

FROM CASTING FOR THE CUTTHROAT (1977)

ADVANTAGE / 25
ALL THOSE WOMEN WANTING TO DIE / 26
CARPE DIEM / 27
CASTING FOR THE CUTTHROAT / 28
HIGH, ALL NIGHT DRIVING TO BERKELEY / 29
MASTERS / 30
THE DISAPPEARANCE OF JOHN / 31
THE SEPARATION / 32
THIS STILLNESS / 34
THOUGHTS FROM A PLANE OVER BIRMINGHAM / 35
TAROT CARD XXI THE WORLD, REVERSED / 36

FROM CASTING FOR THE CUTTHROAT
& OTHER POEMS *(1980)*

1941   / 39
A DAY'S WORK   / 40
THE ART OF POETRY   / 41
AT CODORNICES PARK, BERKELEY   / 42
CRAZY LADY   / 43
CROSSING INTO MEXICO   / 44
DREAM OF LEAVING YOU   / 45
GRAMMAR SCHOOL LESSON   / 46
HOLDING THE INVISIBLE   / 47
IN BIRMINGHAM   / 48
LINE DRAWINGS   / 49
OBJET D'ART   / 50
THE ARTIST   / 51
THE BEST OF FRIENDS   / 52
THE PHOTOGRAPH IS WRONG   / 53
THE WITNESS   / 54
THOUGHTS STOLEN FROM SLEEP   / 55
THREE EVENINGS   / 56
TO A CHILD IN THE RAIN   / 57
YES   / 58

FROM IN THIS HOUR *(1989)*

IN THIS HOUR   / 61
JANUARY, THE DAY YOU DIED   / 62
A MAN   / 63
ALABAMA IN DECEMBER   / 65
APRIL IN ALABAMA   / 67
FLASHBACK   / 68
FOR CALEB   / 70
NEW YEAR'S EVE, SKIING IN TAHOE   / 71

NIGHT IN YOSEMITE VALLEY / 73
SEPARATION / 74
BROWN RABBIT / 75
CONSOLATIONS CONCERNING LEAVING ONE'S GROUND OF BEING / 76
DAY AFTER THE MARKET CRASH / 77
FIGURES, AN INTERPRETATION / 79
FOR A GIRL I ONCE KNEW / 80
FOURTEEN REASONS WHY / 81
HAWAII / 82
HUGO ON CAMPUS / 83
LA BELLE DAME SANS MERCI / 84
LOT'S WIFE / 85
MEDITATION AT POINT REYES / 88
REPORT FROM THOMAS, TEN YEARS AFTER THE ACCIDENT / 90
RIVERSIDE, ALABAMA / 92
FOR NO REASON / 93
BLACKBIRD / 94
FORT MASON BAR, SAN FRANCISCO / 95
HOLD ME / 96
OHLONE PARK, BERKELEY / 97
RUSSIAN RIVER / 98
SEPTEMBER / 99
SEX, GENETICS, THE SEA / 100
UNDER THE PYRAMID BUILDING / 101

NEW WORK

HAY STACKER / 105
POINT PINOLE / 106
THE BEARD / 107
DANA STREET, BERKELEY / 108
THE COMPUTER CONSULTANT'S LAST ASSIGNMENT, CHICAGO / 109
YUBA RIVER TIME / 110
FISHING / 111
CANCER / 112

An Alabama Song / 113
Grace / 114
The Dancers / 115
Climate Change: Drought / 117
Watching You Undress / 118
Three Smiles / 119
Advice / 120
A Lesson on Dying / 121
Joie de Vivre / 122
Three Cows / 123
A New Kind of Weather / 124
The Drowning / 125
Sonata of the Plastic Curtain / 127
Promises to Keep / 128
The Beginning Skier / 129
An Early Morning Surprise / 130
What It's Like / 131
To Remember You / 132
Listening / 133
After Chemo / 134
Losing the Light / 135
Renewal / 136
January / 137

About the Author

FROM *ALL PIECES OF A LEGACY (1975)*

ALABAMA KUDZU

This is the fear, the words
trapped in the back of your throat,
that nothing is enough.
    In your blood you trace
the inner latticework of kudzu,
you understand the brown trees,
all motion pulled to the ground,
like horses drowned in quicksand,
the tall and crumbling pine
beneath an undying green.
    But this is only the fear,
you have told yourself, *regret nothing.*
Your eyes are still blue, and inside
you are still capable of surrendering.

ALL PIECES OF A LEGACY

You receive the memories, the hunger,
and the dreams shiny as the eyes of madmen
before stately antebellum mansions,
even for the poor more than they were,
like lightning bugs stuck to a summer evening.

Patterns like footprints in the grass
of a barefooted run with June bug
on a string, like a child hugged in the arms
of motherhood, tied to a solid, hard-backed green,
the buzzing, broken as first sex in the back of a car.

And you remember the funny talk of poontang
in barber shops before the hunt begins,
the talk of the remorseless chicken thief,
the hungry coon sought after in the night
out beyond the chinaberry tree, the mimosa
and crepe myrtle, out beyond even the dogwood

through the kudzu, hunted and smiling
from the pine tree, smiling at the dogs
pulled with chains from the moon-cut pine;
you remember that trapped and smiling, high-up coon,
you remember the hunger that would not cease, cease.

*A*WAKENING

I can hear the corners of my room touching,
the whole enclosed space leaning around and over me.
I am sealed inside, comfortable and warm, but
I have been out walking;
my hair is still damp with rain
and there is the feel of nearby fog
moving around my feet.
My wool hat smells like a dead animal.

BALLAD

He would be in the forest lifting out
his band-aid box, sandpaper glued to the bottom,
never carried a lighter, and the match would flare:
        the smell of pipe tobacco in the cold winter
air, and I remember him always working, planting,
fishing, walking, a man who distrusted words,
loved his dogs, who would be gone
        hunting all day with his dogs, listening
for the closing of the circle, to his best dog,
listening, leaning with his back against the mossed side,
against some dead old oak.

[for Uncle Bud]

LET'S PLAY A GAME
[from a story told of my grandfather]

Say it was pretend, with a friend, around 1890 or 1910,
  and you've just come home
wearing your flannel shirt that's wet along the cross
  of suspenders on your back.
        Your eyes are wide with shock.
        It was to be playing you were Jesse James
with your one-shot squirrel gun, and you've run
all the way home, leaving behind the sloping hill,
the thick grotto of trees growing up at an angle
to your sense of balance, the one lone oak,
        leaving behind all those twisted dogwoods,
those Christ crooked trees bursting green and white
and the oak with your rope tied just as it was
supposed to be, that grass brown rope
that was your birthday present
        around his neck so blue and bent
hanging from the tree you'd decided was the hanging tree.

BIRMINGHAM

Of all the places you could die
trapped if you didn't leave fast
or have lots of money, this is the one
you remember best. This is your birthplace.
          You wanted out, the day she ran away,
left you the child and the furniture.
But you stayed, innocent and twenty-one,
made love to practiced women. One,
forty-one, who kept your child for free;
one, thirty-three, who hoped her husband
died, a little at a time; and one,
twenty-nine, who came to you animalized,
hardened with lies.
          It was a steel time town, younger
and harder than Birmingham Sunday could break.
Four black children died. You made love
to the wife of a salesman. He failed
to give her children and failed again
she cried when you stopped cold,
told her, no, no more children.
          That night outside Memphis, the Mississippi
mosquitoes like furies bidding you goodbye,
you turn in your mind the meaning of escape.
Almost, you wanted to lie, you're innocent
if you don't go back. The child asleep, your red car
packed, you douse the fire and drive out fast.

COUSIN DINK

I know a man who, at birth,
was broken by a doctor whose hands
faltered in the too long and too hard delivery.
        He grew up broken, his eyes crossed,
his legs withered, his head too large in circumference,
and his whole back scarred from neck to hip.
        He was given one year, two, ten, and now he's thirty,
cousin Dink, with a grade school education,
without bitterness, with scars on his too often burned legs
that have no feeling, and
        would I send him a drinking glass,
the kind you buy at tourist spots, or if not that,
perhaps a road map of California?

*P*ARTING

My father paced me as we shoveled
until I grew tired and watched him
watching me
shoveling
and then when I stopped
he grinned
his feet sinking slowly in the loose dirt
the sweat pouring down his muscled back
in streams.
Somehow he won then
and even as I packed my bags
our angry eyes clashing like iron
and I turned my back on him
I felt that smile
as he shoveled on
past all endurance
that strength of his arms and back
that unworded smile of his disappointment.

MISSOULA SPRING

       I have become
one of my own poems.
This morning
the covered streets
opened black
in melting snow.
       I was wrong.
Winter gone, a flower
opens in me, a song, words
crawl in my veins,
a carnation of the brain,
a dogwood.

MONTANA

The dream of an ashen faced woman wakes me
and it's snowing
and I'm cold.

Her face is hidden
somewhere in shadows,
a phone booth
with one light on
that blinks once
and goes out.

In the dark
the refrigerator cuts on.
I listen to its whine,
the snow falling.

On Your Birthday

I mark it down on my
calendar memory this
Thanksgiving on your
birthday and no presents
except Pat's handmade
tray of recipes;
       and as it grows dark
outside with snow on the
ground all around us the
turkey cooking and the
football game
       I feel suddenly like a
stranger divided between
day and night, who's come
dressed against the cold in
an old shirt, old and full
of holes like a memory.
       And as if I've left my
body drifting in the dark
my hands in you struggle,
relax, and begin slowly to
move again these days like
petals blown before a wind.

for Maggie, in Montana, 1973

IN SAN FRANCISCO

Coming towards me
like light from a distant star
not yet arrived anywhere
he enters the park
fondling an animal-headed
smooth-carved redwood cane;
      then pushing his black
leather jacket loose at the neck
his dark-skinned hand
finds and places the harp,
the black eyes closing,
the coffined chords
a hymn, a dirge,
      and suddenly I know how
the sounds of what I have broken
are healing in the ground.

HAMBURGERS

Billy Watkins
Bird Mill Road
Bogalusa, Miss.

Aug. 5, 1958

Dear Billy,
Just arrived here at the Grand Canyon. What a ditch.
No, really a beautiful place, you should of come. Molly's
standing over my shoulder here, says to tell you, you are the
sweetest brother-in-law a girl ever had and please remember
to water the lawn and lock up. Bogalusa ain't the crime
capital of the world, but you and I both know there's some
will take anything not nailed down.
Car did just fine—Molly says to tell you how Ma and
the kids are having the most fun of their lives—actually they
all been driving me nutsCar did just fine—Molly says to tell
you how Ma and the kids are having the most fun of their
lives—actually they all been driving me nuts - stop here, look
at that, let's all do this. stop here, look at that, let's all do this.
But as I was saying the car's doing just great. Two quarts of
oil is all so far and we been hitting 70 all the way. Told you,
you should have got a Ford when I did. Well, my hand's
getting in a cramp from writing so much, see you when we
get back,

Luke

Billy Watkins
Bird Mill Road
Bogalusa, Miss.

August 8, 1958

Dear Billy,
I don't know how to go about saying this, but last
night after we climbed down to the bottom and back Ma

went to bed real early saying she was just wore out. Well, this morning when we woke up we found that she had passed away during the night. So now we are here at the Holiday Inn in Flagstaff and Ma is laid out on the bed with us and I don't know what we are going to do. God, I sure wish you had a telephone. I keep thinking about Ma. The way she looked riding on top of that old mule, just holding on for dear life. I guess we shouldn't of taken her with us. But she sure wanted to see that Grand Canyon. Well, she saw it and that's that.

Billy, you wouldn't believe what one guy told us on the telephone about how much it costs to send a dead person from Flagstaff to Bogalusa. $500.00 or more! I just don't know what we are going to do. I thought maybe you could ask Hawkins and those guys to try to scrape up some bucks to send us cause I know it's going to cost more than I got on me - I certainly don't have no $500.00 anyway. So, I'm sending you this letter by special delivery and hoping you will get it by tomorrow. I sure hope you do cause I don't know what we're going to do and we sure can't stay here much longer. Molly's going out of her mind the way it is.

Write us and let us know about the money as soon as you're able.

Luke

Billy Watkins
Bird Mill Road
Bogalusa, Miss.

August 10, 1958

Dear Billy,
Just thought you'd like to know we couldn't wait no longer so I took things into my own hands. It was a hell of a mess, but I've got everything under control, everything but

16

Molly that is. She ain't done nothing but cry and tell me what a sacrilege I'm making. Hell, there wasn't nothing else could be done. Those people at the Holiday Inn were just getting to the point we couldn't keep them out of our room no longer. So I've taken that tarp, you remember the one I got from the mill, wrapped her up in it and tied her to the top of the car. It was real funny though. After I brought the tarp in I couldn't look at her no more. I just had to turn my head. And then after I got her wrapped and waterproofed and went to pick her up, it was like there wasn't anything to her, like in dying all the weight had been taken out of her. Hell, I couldn't even tell she was in there.

Anyway, we're planning to check out of this place in an hour or so and then drive twenty hours a day until we get home. Should be about day after tomorrow. So, I would appreciate it if you would get the funeral all set up for the day after we get back. I guess that'd be Thursday.

Luke

P.S. Sorry we couldn't wait no longer for the money, but we just had to do something. Billy, this is being real hard on all of us. I sure hope you got things ready when we get there. Now, on top of everything else it looks like it's going to rain.

Billy Watkins
Bird Mill Road
Bogalusa, Miss.

August 12, 1958

Dear Billy,
There must be a curse on us Watkins. I don't know how else to explain what's gone wrong. We drove all night

last night and by this afternoon when we hit Little Rock we seemed to have it licked. We went through three rain storms and with all this heat, Molly afraid she's smelling something all the way, and the kids screaming that they're starving to death, we decided to stop and rest for awhile. So, when we saw this big Hamburgers sign at that truckstop right off the highway, we parked in the back and all of us run inside without looking back once.

The car was just running great and I figured we could make it home in under six hours the way things were going, so we just sat there, none too anxious to go back to the car you understand, for about two hours. And when we did, my God, Billy, she was gone. No sight of her anywhere, car and all. It was stolen, Billy. Some fucking bastard stole my car. So now we are here stranded at the police station in Little Rock. Course I didn't tell them about Ma. Just reported my car as stolen. But I keep wondering what those bastards are going to do when they find what else they've stolen. Billy, I been thinking about it, and I don't think we're ever going to see her again. I think we had better just keep this whole thing to ourselves and go on with a funeral service as if nothing at all is the matter.

Anyway, the police here say they reckon we can hitch a ride with a prison van going over to Sharkey tomorrow. We can wait for you there, okay? We can figure out more of what to tell people then.

Billy, it just keeps going over and over in my head, if only we hadn't stopped for those goddam hamburgers. And I keep thinking of Ma sitting up there holding on to that long eared mule. I just don't understand how so much could go wrong in such a short time.

See you in Sharkey.

Luke

THE PALACE OF NEW BEGINNINGS

Alison wanted to believe that words made no difference, but words were her weakness. She had agreed to see him.

She stared at the snow. The apartment grew cold. The couch suddenly became ugly, a brown that made no sense, wouldn't ever die out, a brown she watched spreading around her, holding the room to the carpet. At first it was like drowning in air, a slipping inside oneself feeling the darkness close as though a zipper were being shut. But then like a wave leveling back into the body of a lake, her emotions retreated. The couch remained a thing of cushions and legs, a matter of ordinary experience. Outside it continued to snow.

Alison Benet was thirty-three. She had one child, David Benet, and was now separated from her husband, John David Benet. It was midnight, but even so she decided to bathe and wash her hair. John would be coming tomorrow. She began to undress where she stood. The snow would not stick. Tomorrow would be a mess. Her body tingled from the chill in the room. Yes, she had grown thin. She lifted one breast and examined it, let it fall. Her body seemed a separate thing to her, something that lived, breathed, felt of its own will. It had not always been so. She had been young once. When? How long ago? She stared at the veins just visible, coursing blue tracks, her breast rising with her breathing. John would be coming. For an instant his large face on the pillow. She had been young once. Tomorrow he was coming. No, she did not hate him. All at once she wanted to laugh. Why had she agreed to see him? Because she needed to see him again, she thought, once more, know him, know his hands on her, know for the last time he meant nothing to her.

#

John David rises alone. It's early morning. The clatter of his dressing fills the cabin. Tennis shoes padding to a

19

square kitchen sink. In a mirror the size of his hand he brushes his teeth, splashes water at his face. It's cold, ice cold. He smiles. His large face does not fit the mirror. Two rows of teeth, pieces of grinning cheek, open large nostrils bring him the morning.

Outside he begins to run. One lap of the lake. Three miles. It has taken him two months to build up to it. The right distance, he has decided: enough given, enough taken away. The cottonwoods around the lake loom up stark and pale out of the white morning. He crosses the ruins of a barbed wire fence, descends a small incline, and begins to run again. Soon the heavy snow will come. The lake will freeze over and his routine will be broken. But for now, again he settles into the pace. The muffled steps of his running lift into stillness.

A slow warmth spreads through his arms and legs. His glasses grow opaque in the cold. He knows this path. Barren, half-white trees lift over him dripping with snow. He runs, half-perceived images striking at the edges of his vision, and the outside world of lake, trees, and snow begins to slip away. He will be with her in a few hours. They have been separated almost three months now. Why does he want to see her again? Why did he talk her into it? He imagines her running naked before him in the snow. He wants her. He can't help himself. In his mind he is chasing her, but she is like a bird, pretends she is hurt, leading him away from something, something she does not want him to find. And he follows her, her heavy blond hair over her back, laughing at him now, he wants her, his breath coming faster, the way she dances, and suddenly he is running and she is afraid. He will take her now. She cannot last and he is running flat out, he will have her, flat out into nothingness.

Where the path curves back to his cabin he comes to a halt. Immediately he is cold. Overhead a shaftless arrow of ducks going South. Suddenly Alison is a reality again.

#

She placed two blouses on her bed—David had spent the night with his grandparents—and walked to the window wearing jeans and sandals. Already the snow was melting. It remained piled only in shadows. The coffee pot began crackling on the stove. She poured herself a second cup, but did not drink any, returned to her bedroom and rejected the Mexican print for the white silk. Then, before the mirror, tortoiseshell rose tinted glasses, peacock feather earrings, no bra, her blond hair tied in a loose braid, she thought, *It's not a matter of deception, but of pleasure. Why did it take me so long to discover that?* She returned to her coffee, but it was cold. She poured it out, turned the burner on low; he would be arriving any minute now. She sat down to wait.

#

John David Benet roared to a stop before the florist's shop, raced the engine once and turned it off. For a moment he seemed a night rider, a vision of death and destruction. Off came his black mask, his rain suit glistening, and he ran inside to return with a dozen long-stemmed roses. Then even the roar of his cycle seemed the expression of something gentle, a dream discovered to be reality, a simple man on a simple journey.

#

At the door to her apartment he suddenly became nervous. A presentiment. She would refuse him. In a rush he saw it all. She would be dressed up, the apartment clean, and David would be gone, staying with her parents again. It was a set-up. She would refuse him. He looked down at his clothes. They seemed baggy and ill-formed. Behind the door she would be waiting, beautiful, waiting for him to try something, waiting to refuse him. He felt ridiculous. He wanted to put on his rain suit again, his helmet, rush through the door and attack her as she stood with her hand still stretched out to him. Suddenly he wanted to leave, sneak down the stairs, and leave. She would refuse him. That thought spinning around and around finally dropped inside him like an anchor. He felt it sinking, felt the line grow taut, and placing his motorcycle gear on the floor, lifting the roses before him, he knocked on the door. On hearing the rustle of her approach, a hot wave rushed at his face.

The roses in a blue vase between them, they seemed unable to find the right tack for conversation.

"How's David?" he said, and looked around the room as though expecting to find him hidden somewhere, his gaze finally coming to rest on a tiny racing car wedged under the credenza.

"He's fine," she said. "He wanted to spend the night with my parents." There was a tone of self-defense to her voice which she did not like.

He smiled, grimly.

And then, "You're looking beautiful today," without looking at her, the words like a challenge. And he could not look at her, her nipples clearly visible beneath the silk, noticed the racing car was missing a wheel, wanted to take down her hair, run his hands under her breasts, was grateful for the roses between them.

And she accepted the challenge. She *was* beautiful today. She knew it, knew it as a pleasure that tingled inside her, knew he could not look at her, knew it and reached forward, pushed the roses over to one side, said, "Well now, let me have a look at you."

FROM *CASTING FOR THE CUTTHROAT (1977)*

ADVANTAGE

In France beside some shabby old wall
the water runs dirty with sunlight
and I walk, moss-brown stones beneath my feet,
toward you with open arms. You are blond now.
You have changed only the color of your hair.
All the rest remains the same.
          In your eyes I see you don't understand,
as if you're puzzled by my greeting. Being polite
you invite me to coffee before finding you're afraid:
there are no witnesses. Always we are alone.
It's then you begin to doubt, and I discover
once again how your grave face will unravel
          remembering when we were young,
when your dark hair glistened like a river in the sun.

ALL THOSE WOMEN WANTING TO DIE

No longer takes me by surprise.
        The heavy magic of dreamers
sometimes self-destructs; only their words
are left behind. The body floats away,
        a black coach in January air, a wind
over coastal mountains, returning home,
zephyrs, ciphers,
        like frail shadows
before the light goes out.

CARPE DIEM
for Maggie

You can't find your shoes.
    Exiting your closet as from the insides
of a civilization you stand in the ruins:
all the etcetera of a lifetime: your huge
black Cadillac of a baby carriage, slide
projector, vacuum cleaner, umbrella . . .
    but not the shoes you need.
    You enter the bathroom without looking back,
slip into a hot tub of water. Your eyes seethe
brown with wickedness over your body. The suds
have crept to your hair.
    With a breath, your breasts float high
in the gray water.
    You are alive.
    You become, slowly, the woman's body
you understand, your own, and
    you know when you step from the tub,
wet and warm-red, with
    pieces of dreams still molten inside you,
    how porcelain your world can become.

CASTING FOR THE CUTTHROAT
for Richard Hugo

He sneaks after some woman who could not love him,
a woman from his school days, who would never love him.
He knew it, snaking like a thief after the praise
from her lips, like a fisherman casting
only for the cutthroat, living
out his years forever dumb
before this woman who could touch him,
thinking only the barrenness of Garnet,
Montana, could cure him,
this madness that could not be cured,
his own special madness,
the way the green of a river bank
reminds him of her,
the way she's always young as porcelain
and he's grown old, his books
like school houses ablaze in the snow.

HIGH, ALL NIGHT DRIVING TO BERKELEY

Drink beer, follow the headlights,
the highway knows where a woman waits
who loves me. Drunks pass on by;
all maniacs stay in bed; I'm high
and Berkeley's near with its strong
ocean-like ways. The desert behind, a song
plays in my ear. Already sea waves run white
lines one at a time down the moonlit night.
Your tides pull me along; your curve of thigh
runs in my mind; your round brown eyes
close once again. Take me, take me, says the song;
the maps show I can make no wrong
decisions. Home, to know your body as before;
I am a desert-wrecked-dreamer come to shore.

MASTERS

I pick you out, a man to become,
yes and no together; you lead me
into the desert. Your single words
are too thick for meaning. I
can't make them out. The cactus
plants are all I understand. And
the heat.
In the moment I look around
you fall behind: whose death
do I feel? This is all a dream.
I wake, think of writing it down.
A man walks in thru my window
from Montana. "Thirty white geese
are saved from extinction," he says,
helps himself to my liquor.
We ignore the snow.
I was just in Mexico," I say,
did you feel something die?" He rages out
in the midst of a blizzard, with my liquor.
This is another dream. The white petals
all sink to the ground in a row.

THE DISAPPEARANCE OF JOHN

A young woman is working over her husband.
He's becoming a statue. She hammers away, shouting,
"John, John, I know you can hear me. John?"
      But even as she hammers, he's slipping
into stone. He is not escaping, he knows
the blood is ceasing to flow, replaced
bit by bit by stone.
      Already his eyes appear to be fading,
that feverish glow of anxiety gone. "John?
Are you in there?" and the chisel in haste
placed just center of the shoulder blades,
"John?"
      Staring at the resultant dust
on her kitchen floor, she stamps her foot,
"John, this has gone too far!"
before she sweeps him up, and stores
what remains in a silver jar.

THE SEPARATION

It happened a sleepless evening after one of her parties, as though she'd been waiting for him. She felt strangely deserted, her husband asleep, the servants gone, and her house seemed to vibrate like a tuning fork set below the range of human hearing. A wind had come up. She paced the floors listening, and suddenly he was there. Young. Blond. The feel of an abandoned child in his eyes, the slight fuzz of a beard on his cheeks.

At first she wanted to call the police, but she couldn't bring herself to do it. Light seemed to gather around his face. A new feeling rose inside her. As though she'd taken a lover. And so he remained. She allowed it.

From behind the lace curtains of her upstairs window, she watched him pee into the gardenia bush. It was the simplicity of his acts, she decided, that fascinated her so. Secretly, she mapped the range and hour of his small excursions into her garden. She knew what he ate, when and where he relieved himself. The smallest of his movements took on an exaggerated importance. To know he was on the grounds was a comfort to her.

It was early one cold morning, a light snow on the ground, she began to worry about him. A darkness had gathered in his face. He seemed suddenly somewhat emaciated. True, lately, she had ignored him, but ... It occurred to her she should go down to him. She couldn't bring herself to do it.

That evening she dreamed she stood over a pool of stagnant water, stirred with a thick stick, lazy brown goldfish, each with the face of her child. All slowly dying. She woke up screaming.

Her nightgown raised to her knees, she ran out to him.

His face had become like chalk. His eyes were empty.

She kneeled beside him, almost touched him, and for the first time he seemed about to speak. She leaned closer.

His mouth fell open with a sudden bright flaming. A wind rushed over them as the house watched them lift from the ground. Lace curtains reached out for her. Her husband sat up in his bed. The echo of her name banged through his empty house.

THIS STILLNESS

As she goes up the stairs, suddenly
I remember a river I once watched
rushing powerful and dark after a long rain.
  Her shoulders seem thin and spare.
I stare at her thighs softly splotched
with white paint. Two canvases tonight.
Fatigue rests in her eyes. She says good night.
  Overhead a jet rumbles through the dark,
cars pass in the street. I listen as she undresses.
The children sleep. And I remember the river:
  how it seemed strangely unfamiliar, becoming
a remorseless, ceaseless roar, taking everything
within its reach; and I sat beside it on the bank, arms
around my knees, holding this stillness inside me.

THOUGHTS FROM A PLANE OVER BIRMINGHAM

My mother sick, the plane drifts
years, banking for landing, and suddenly
I'm home.
    And the orange, industrialized sky
still says the furnaces are working overtime,
steel from the steel-born town.
    The stewardess shakes the sleepers awake,
engines rev, landing gear down, and the home
I thought I'd left behind returns
as we touch the ground. Home
    because what's free was never born,
because what opens at the beginning remains
open till the end.

TAROT CARD XXI THE WORLD, REVERSED

Now,
old refusals come out of the ground like swords;
they went unrecognized for years.

I watch the freeway traffic and think of home,
not the real one, but the one I imagined
where failures were forgotten.

I have weaved the clothes of a castaway
believing expectations I filled
would fulfill my needs.

How easy to continue even when it's wrong,
when momentum carries me like sleep:
and I need only to quit,

to sit silent
with one word
brewing in my mouth.

1941

Arriving in the parking lot
the evening I'm born, he stands
hands in his empty pockets,
fresh from a high school
that never taught him anything
about anything except fighting
and the war going on,
and knows that green sea of wall lockers
is behind him. It is August
and the black pavement still steams
with rain. Staring up
the high brick wall and windows
he tries to guess which one I'm in,
not yet believing there is one,
those square yellow lights like sleep
and a dream he can't wake up from.

A Day's Work

For so little pay
to move all day with that weight
slung backwards and watch the dust
cover my hands like a new skin,
to stagger behind a black man who pulls
forward like a horse in harness,
so much power in his arms and back,
to lift that white substance from the plant,
that feeling of the seeds stuck in the center,
to stuff cotton balls in one smooth motion
without breaking stride
till it's sundown beside the oak
beneath a red-varnished sky,
and an old man plopped down beside me,
wiping his eyes, face dust brown as mine,
saying, "Damn wind done made me cry."

THE ART OF POETRY

Once more, buddy, your last ride
has left you behind and nothing can be done.
You want someone to come, a silver angel,
to seize your hair and lift you from the earth.
        But the weight of your two feet
presses against the ground. No one comes
to save you. It's too cold to stand still
and too dark to run.
        Once more, buddy, you write
to save yourself. Here's the barn.
Here the horses are warm. Here, on a dark
night, between towns, between meals,
simply the heat of other animals is enough.

AT CODORNICES PARK, BERKELEY

for Bruce Hawkins
poet and Sunday morning guard

And when pores open, legs pumping,
I see that his court awareness still survives,
a forty-year-old four-eyes who understands
this language of fast breaks and fingertip
finesse, the backdoor pass and give and go,
and easy lay-ups.
            Because here is control
and that fun of full extension,
the face and flush of perfect
pick and roll. Because his hands
are filled with suggestions.
Because always his inscrutable sentences
begin in the arc of a hook shot.
            And the ball falls, spinning backwards
a prescribed imagistic route,
a will creating its own reasons
for grinning: sunlight, trees,
this irrevocable letting go
of what is already falling,
that sense of sweetest swish
thru unbroken string.

CRAZY LADY

Only dreams and sweet revenge from a soft
romance—someone stole her baby. Dilated
eyes now search your face. Was it you?
A judge declared it best, and so look, here's to elegance
    and extravagance
and her tough beauty on the streets.
        But today she's not high enough;
she feels the parenthesis of her sex
closing over emptiness. She moves
to hold you fast, poised at the edge of herself.
You have to make everything simple,
she says; align things by ones
before you divide.
        But touch no more than her
thin bare arms and a light comes on inside her,
and then a toast, here's to her Byzantine beauty,
and a home away from home, sweet San Francisco,
here's to where she sleeps in the streets,
and her mouthtalker, eyeseer poetry.

CROSSING INTO MEXICO

We come here as tourists
thinking of Aztecs in the interior
and discover the border towns,
houses made from Coca-Cola signs,
homes built from the scrap of an empire
next door.
Here failure becomes real
in the uncurious outstretched hands
of children, where our cheap yellow Fiat
leaps like a coin in the sun.
When we leave these towns
I think of Trotsky, the man with an axe
in his head, of Zapata and his silver white stallion,
but before us is the desert, a desert
that knows nothing of hope,
and I am almost grateful for the emptiness,
the illusory lakes rising and falling
over the highway.

DREAM OF LEAVING YOU

This dream about leaving you
begins with your clothes on the floor
and flowers falling from your hair;

then there's an icy drink
at my elbow and the air
of a conversation that will not end,

the way time sits in your mouth
like cold sunshine and doors
wink open around you.

GRAMMAR SCHOOL LESSON
for Demian

Said, "Dad, could you help me a minute?"
your math book laid out on the table.
Nothing easier, percentages, fractions,
        but then your tears ruined
all my answers, thinking words like "exacerbate"
and "patience."
        How events appear like conjugations of verbs:
wanting to help, needing to be helped,
hating of the helper, punishment of the helped.
        My life feels like an equation,
the way your hands are shaped
exactly like mine.

HOLDING THE INVISIBLE

Meaning,
holding those things which can not be seen,
which I can not show you,
the way a vase tilts inside me
when you walk by,
the way we've lived in each other's lives
as if it made no difference,
a breath of air,
the wind in the curtains,
the way we come together in the dark,
that feeling of something falling,
my outstretched hands.

IN BIRMINGHAM

for Annie Newton-Allison

Grandma is home from the hospital.
They couldn't kill her, she says, the way
they killed her son, Bud. The dead are so many
and so far behind.
   She remembers the Depression, how Bud
had done the work of ten, not because he was stronger,
but because he was smarter, never wasted a thing
in his life. Dead, too, her husband who always wore
starched shirts because there were no excuses
before God, and her children who hadn't survived
childhood. It's everything and yet it's nothing,
nearly blind from cataracts, who recalls
her own grandfather come home to die who wrote
strange songs and poems on the backs of paper bags,
worthless words and another mouth to feed.
   Her mother was an ignorant woman, she says,
and asks if we know about the caves near Bridgeport.
There are bones there, she's heard, artifacts
that go back two thousand years. She says she remembers
Birmingham before the streets were paved. It's everything
and yet it's nothing. In the backyard she's had
a pecan planted to replace the fig. The tree
had worn itself out, she says; it had stopped
bearing fruit.

LINE DRAWINGS

1
Although it is you
the artist does not see you.
The line remains flat,
no more than surface,
a figure without shadow or depth.
Yet it is you;
that is your face
showing the uncertainty, your pose,
and the artist draws something
almost whole and defined
before giving up, before
the map of your bones
is forgotten, before the years
of his training take over.
His lines have their own reasons;
his hand pleasures in itself.

2
The way thought removes itself
in times of conflict, the line
remembers only line. Intention
disappears. The way she becomes
again, without clothes, a nude,
this woman, breasts tilted upward,
captured here in her attitude
of turning away from all of us
who might have known her,
hand draped over hip
in defiance and invitation,
yet giving up, as if the world
only imagined her, discovered
for the first time her face
and the guilt, the unseeing smile,
each line beginning her loosening shape,
her body spread out,
emptied and available.

OBJET D'ART

In the beginning
there was a feeling of being found,
discovered,
the way he fit so neatly inside her
world view of things,
his appearance as it were,
and the armature of his being
becoming by necessity the base
which best displayed her beauty
so alarmingly.

THE ARTIST

for John Mullen

Everyone is an artist, he said,
inside. Inside there is someone
very, very old, someone only
an ancestor would recognize,
someone sheltered in a doorway
singing songs in a dew-dropping cold,
singing songs we always seem to know
as if we'd heard the words long, long ago.

THE BEST OF FRIENDS
for Lee Fesperman

In the East Bay mud
ride black rubber tires;
through tide after tide
they surface, glistening
with night's viscous reward
for wearing out.
Long-eyed rodents
mount them in the dark
and wait the coming of dawn.
Like someone playing
the piano, divertimento,
something ends,
can not be started again.

THE PHOTOGRAPH IS WRONG
for Janice

It was on a chert-red road near Birmingham,
our weathered gray farm house tilting
toward the earth. Green fingers of kudzu
had claimed the chimney and roof.
    When I look closely I can make out
railroad beds and a field of dead grass
in the distance. It was taken in Indian summer.
You are sitting under the mimosa trees, looking
like life has been good to you. It wasn't true.
    That was the year it snowed, a false spring
bloom on everything. I remember pointing to the trees,
saying how beautiful they were, undressed that way
and standing in ice.

THE WITNESS

The need for perfection and
the mounting failures
and distractions
fill your clothes, yet
like the witness in poetry
reporting on what was seen,
nothing more,
the song, the rhythm, the plot,
and nothing more, you see
only the vision and,
like the reason for eating, feel it
necessary,
living.

Thoughts Stolen from Sleep

The snow on a branch in winter
and iron pipes wrapped against the cold,
these feelings are like sleeping while awake,
the selves you wrap up in, the thefts
you render smaller and smaller until
they begin to disappear, like small
lead bullets lodged in your heart,
no damage, no epiphany, only
a kind of icy clarity,
a metaphor that feeds upon itself,
the whole range of your experience,
the sound of it!

THREE EVENINGS

I. Snow lies along the edge
of the road, peeled away
like birch-bark parchment.

I try to tell you
only what's on my mind,
but my words have no sound
on their own, and the cold
settles in the corners
of the house.

II. It has begun to rain.
The drain rattles with water
to the ground. I sit at the window,
watch the pines bend with the wind,
the snow as it begins to sink.

Only one voice refuses to give in;
I listen as a crow calls
and calls again.

III. This evening there is sunlight
in the pine straw and a heavy,
whispery breeze on the hilltops.
Everything feels emptied.

There is nothing to say.
Decisions are like aspens and birch,
speaking when no one's listening.

To a Child in the Rain

It was to play in the rain
you took off your clothes,
damned the gutter's river,
Red Mountain's water down Birmingham
streets, the way you could lie back
and be carried away, naked,
in the wet wash of summer rain,
and no plans but to swim down the river,
your street, become the world you lived in,
the fire tower and mountain top,
the mimosa and oak, as if the horizon
could reach down and touch you
like a sweeping brush stroke,
and you belonged to the landscape,
like sidewalk cracks and mud, the way
the tiny glass horses you held
remained rearing and alive
in their milky white light.

YES

We were waiting in a stand of pines. The hounds announced themselves. *Yes*, he said, *yes, they'll cross over there.* And he began to run.

I remember catching up, my uncle taking the pistol from his clothes as he knelt on the road. It had rained earlier that morning and the smoke stayed close to the ground, the sound burning in my ears.

Yes, he said, *fine rabbit if he doesn't have worms,* and he smiled, his hand once again disappearing beneath his coat.

And the rabbit was so small, shot through the head, and I was amazed and puzzled, a child knowing that shot was a feat of perfection somehow. So small and he had shot it from so far away.

So small, and yes, he had stood there holding it by the ears, the wind bending around us, the trees singing the song of what could be remembered, but never again touched.

FROM *IN THIS HOUR (1989)*

IN THIS HOUR

Even in the fog and dark wind
I can feel the tide coming in,
the steady wash and swell,
and sea salt along the shore,
and I try to make myself empty
to no avail.
   Somewhere ahead I imagine
an avenging angel, one of swift
shadow and sure ending, and I can
almost feel its beating wings,
a predator breaking from cover
in full autumn sail.
   But for now in this hour
the sea's lapping continues and
it's like an animal breathing
against the beach. I listen with each
light touch of the surf, and my hand
moves inside your silence, inside
your life and body's warmth.

JANUARY,
THE DAY YOU DIED

for my first wife, Janice Kirkpatrick Entrekin, 1943-1966

Back and forth to work
reading *Wuthering Heights,*
on the bus with Catherine
and Heathcliff, umbrellas,
five o'clock faces and I see,
I see you in the street,
wine-colored skirt, blue tennis
sneakers, stepping from the curb
past the corner of my eye—horns
and the open door, rush hour
traffic. Everywhere wet hair,
the black ordinary coats,
a flower store. Never there.
A small dog barks. Distant.
A trick of the mind to see you today
in California, so many years into darkness,
and under the awning, standing
beside a can of white, gold-centered
daisies, I no longer ask why. Rain
dances the sidewalks. It's Wednesday.
We have nothing to say.

A MAN

for Grandpa Allison

Dawn, and in this September morning the old man watched the mists swirl thickly the length of his creek, the earth spongy and dark. He had walked a muddied path to the water's edge and then moved, a pale white figure clothed in Sunday black, through the mist toward the pasture and his bottom land. Out of the quiet came the occasional flat tone of a cow bell, one of his own. He walked without hurry. And with his staff, a thick dried vine he had cut for himself, he poked at the rotted timbers as he passed.

The old man came to a stop where the rotted logging bridge had stood. It lay collapsed under the water's swirl. The creek was high, backed up, foamy with scum. It seemed to flow in reverse. Brown, sawdust colored froth gathered and circled on the surface. He turned and started around the flooded, muddied ground when a cottonmouth slipped from a limb off to his left.

The hushed wet slap of its body went through him like a chill. He stood for a moment and stared at the off-yellow shading just visible across its throat. Then he stepped over a deadfall and blocked its path to the creek.

A log on either side, the moccasin backed, then stopped and coiled. There was a hollow snapping noise. The mouth gaped open displaying the white gullet. The old man stabbed at it with his staff. His eerie, high pitched voice echoed briefly in the damp woods as he laughed.

When the snake lurched forward, the old man almost lost his footing, his white hair flapping down into his eyes. He stepped quickly to one side and his staff crashed heavily across the tail. The snake boiled immediately into a writhing mass that abruptly disappeared down the bank into the water.

The old man stared. Nothing. Rings widened across the surface, bent, then broke beneath the foam. Something else that would not be finished flared from inside him. Suddenly he was gasping. He could not get his breath. He staggered away from the water into a hollow of thorns and scrub. Then he sat down and stopped, leaned back against a mossed-over oak.

His eyes seemed unfocused, and yet in the twilight of this morning, hands by his side, he was still briefly alive in his life as he watched the dragon flies before him mating in midair. And as he listened for the children running in his blood, he stared out through the rising mists at a glistening, pale white sun. For a moment it remained there, like something that was melting inside him. Then it was gone.

ALABAMA IN DECEMBER

1.

First day back, Birmingham, in the dark basement
of my father's house, standing below
ground looking up: old Mason Jars,
opaque Coca-Cola bottles, one window;
outside in this too warm December,
the newly budding pink of azalea blossoms;
and I can still feel my mother's hand
from early morning, shaking,
the children afraid of her now,
her closeness to death, dark veins
tracking the dry swamp of her skin,
shaking.

In a thin winter sweater I wander
outside under the close Southern sun,
my feet walking my father's land,
feel again the way pine, oak,
ironwood form a stand,
the ground gone a dusty ochre
brown, dead, red leaves
holding forth from a single tree.

Footprints. Relatives in every direction.
Like creeks, rivers, graves:
this family.

2.

Afternoon, in the dim bedroom light,
I watch as her shaking stops,
and starts her staring, far off
into a world of her own, all bones
and soft transparent flesh. As she drifts,

her thin arms move, hands grip at the bed
as if to take hold once again the edge
of her bridge back before sleep.

In the quiet dark I remember playing
in Red Mountain's forests and mines,
how we invented ways out,
nightmares climbing up behind us
out of the muck, and the white sightless fish
we found, trapped in the iron-red water
of an underground lake.

And later, like a plane leaving the ground,
I remember those curving shapes, those blind
creatures suddenly visible in our light,
as real as the gentle bed of lilies she grew
one year, as real as the life we shared,
and yes, that was happy,
that life, when I could walk all the way home
with my eyes closed.

APRIL IN ALABAMA

for Ruth, my mother, who died after a 15-year
battle with Parkinson's disease

My father once shouted that she loved me best.
Now, again he stares without seeing, and yes,
I know he thinks I have her feel on me still.
Always she was so quiet, insisting without speaking,
always seeming to know she gave context, shape,
thickness to things.

And now her relations have arrived, her grandchildren,
dressed up, stage-whispery voices, this
quiet sobbing punctuating the sunny morning,
with a pack of Marlboros left on an end table,
coffee, truck roars from a nearby freeway,
and me, just in from California, like an unholy
ear, listening.

In chapel we sit with silent faces, dark
mahogany walls closing in. A hoarse cough
of a relative with a cold, echoes.

Outside I see kudzu clings, covers new leaves.
Spring. Even as Alabama forests hold
onto a muddy, monochromatic brown
there is a new business in this humid air,
wasps, dirt-daubers, bees.

Afterwards, with everyone gone, with the wind
I feel her out there, like fish and mosquitoes,
lakes, blowing grass, dead leaves, dung beetles,
and, yes, the bees.

FLASHBACK
for Janice

In San Francisco the surf pounds
and I stand quite still,
the shaking of the car now inside me,
and I remember her walking toward the highway
to Memphis, her back and shoulders bent forward
into her gray unreasonableness,
the hard edge of her gentle denials:
only going out to be alone, alone
for a walk, for a walk by herself,
and surely I could understand.
     It was over twenty years ago:
she was not coming back; she was leaving,
wearing her smiles and refusals,
her firmness after so many failures.
And still my dumb hands wanted
to hold her, but she peeled them loose,
and it was snowing, and there were
large wet flakes on her face.
     It was the beginning of winter;
I wasn't ready, I was outside my body
looking down into the dark,
green watercress under the culvert;
a thin film of ice covered the roads;
and I remember seeing myself standing there,
rush hour traffic backed up for miles,
her note folded in my hand.
There was nothing I could have said;
she wasn't there; she was nowhere, pale and still,
lost in the silence of the snowfall,
in the cold air, gone, the flash of a leaping fish
in the distance.
     And I remember how it was, floating
up above the cars and trucks, weightless
over the old country road, and nothing to be done,
only me, the phone man's son, floating
in the slow flood of an evening light,

the policeman waving everyone on, the flashing
red lights over her stark white face,
and no answers as I floated on,
between lives.
　　　　Between then and now,
here on an early winter's day, standing
beside the Great Highway,
just south of the Cliff House, remembering,
watching as the sun is suffused
with magenta and orange,
that indifferent engine of light, magnificent
as it turns below the waves.

FOR CALEB

Who sits in my car and tells me
he's not afraid; twelve now,
he explains how all his friends' parents
are divorced,
and I think how ferociously he played soccer
today, and suddenly I am afraid.
I don't want it to happen, for
the coming days of my absence
to become a lost language.
          Caleb, listen, I remember nights
standing by your bed before sleep,
before you even knew I was possible,
and I knew for the second time
that I was not alone. And I remember you
on the slopes, skiing, when you,
bending far down into a tuck
as we raced for the bottom, laughed
out loud in the gathering speed.
And giving into it, I went with you,
leaning into the wind.
          I will never let you go
out of my life. Listen, Caleb,
just as it was that day,
skiing down the mountain,
even in full flight
a way always opens at our feet.

NEW YEAR'S EVE, SKIING IN TAHOE
for Demian

This night heading north
we slosh upwards, behind
windshield wipers, climbing
into darkness towards the snow,
leaving behind the glittering oil refineries
of Richmond, like space stations in the cold kindling air,
and taking one thing at a time,
I say nothing,
listen to Sting,
"The Blue Turtle's Dream,"
listen to the night
as it becomes colder, lighter,
losing itself in the headlights.
        A morning like this, I think,
rising up through the man-made meadows,
firs at my feet, mists and cold
snowlight spreading time out in pieces,
as we dangle in the dappled light, underground streams
    of water breaking
through ice, and I am in love with my life,
even in the muffled gruff wind,
flat slap of impact, cries
of crashing skiers in the snow.
        For an instant the mountain shrugs
with this string of us on its back; we sway,
suddenly stilled, then jerk ahead,
snug in the cable's grip.
        In that tingling of pain, my feet
becoming stone, I hold halfway down
the mountain side as everyone stops to watch this just
    grown man, my son, Demian,
stoop, then fly maniacally straight down
The Chute, straight down, zooming,
nearly a blur in the distance, and I feel
momentarily as if I have been sealed inside the walls
    of my life, mute
as an empty bell as he flashes past,

shouting and screeching back to earth
in a rooster tail of snow.
        In the warm car we climb
Donner Pass; far above us cottony dark clouds
swirl over the landscape, and still
there are echoes in the mists, of skiers,
fallen and alone. Far below us,
in stone, Donner Lake slips away, placid
as black glass.

NIGHT IN YOSEMITE VALLEY

I have come back weary,
stand with wet hair after a shower,
in moonlight, in the massive blackness
of Cathedral rock rising up behind us,
blocking the stars.
         Here something holds me to the earth.
I move slowly, awake to glass-like granite
and boulders born a million years ago,
to the quick flitting in the gloaming of bats,
and I feel the planet's deaths,
how they have come and gone, the seasons
like the quick breaths of a saxophone,
and my own life suddenly stills.
         Listen, I want only to slip reasonably
out from the trees, cross meadows in the darkness,
sneak past the shy deer and colorful backpackers,
climb up to the snow line. Tonight I know the open
moon, and the city lights that blink up and down
the freeways call to someone else. I am alive.
My childhood sparks like a filament in the dark.

SEPARATION

It's night now.
I'm going out,
stand beneath a redwood tree,
in a Berkeley backyard, listen
to a neighbor's clothes dryer,
tick of metal buttons,
wait for what I left behind,
things I don't know about,
clothes I once wore, beginning
even here in this line,
to leave me, disappear
like a memory, turning
discontinuous, folding
in the night inside me.

BROWN RABBIT
in my Berkeley backyard

Found under the hutch
in the rain, the extended
long legs and ears, wet smell
of rabbit shit, and I remembered
how they thump the ground hard in warning,
  this one strangely fit,
nothing broken, stopped still in its
attitude of running, midair,
this frozen loneliness in its legs
out-leaping whatever had run her
to ground.

CONSOLATIONS CONCERNING
LEAVING ONE'S GROUND OF BEING
after a painting by Ross Drago

Head back, eyes
fixed straight ahead,
this skinny carpenter
has climbed to the top
of his canvas; he's
trying to get out.

Hammer raised for a blow
that never comes, he's
stopped there. He's not
coming down. What was broken
will remain broken
in some other life. Now,
all his problems are one.

Yes, I think, this is the ladder
of dreams, that chain of reasoning
from which, once begun, no one
escapes.

Still it's satisfying how we go,
one by one, like equations,
sealing ourselves off, prepared
like cows, three stomachs, to live
anywhere. We build our own case;
ascend into it.

DAY AFTER THE MARKET CRASH
SAN FRANCISCO, OCTOBER, 1987

The spare change saxophone player
at Market and Sansome
holds sway over the pink
gray day, and five o'clock
faces in pin striped suits, and
a young man and his girl, sipping beer
beside the bank's imitation Greek patio,
its concrete columns roofed with glass.

As if in a dream, his sound comes from
inside a cacophony of commuters at day's end,
from all the transients in this corner of the city,
the weasely newspaper vendor, the birdlike
yelps and yells of bicycle messengers, their
punk red hair, warlike warnings subtly fading
into air, as suddenly from inside it all,
the spare change saxophone player blows, leaning back,
knees bent, eyes closed, into the hollow of the bank's
echoes. A Mississippi melody.
A sound of innocence lost,
echoes.

And at the periphery of being alive, an unfolding
begins, and this random audience stops
inside its life of rushing elsewhere, stops;
steps outside the scheme of things. The newspapers say
the economy is collapsing. But not for now; for now,
even though Rumplestiltskin is working
spinning straw into gold, it makes no difference.
For they have stopped to listen to dreams
older than their own, and those that can
swim in this tide of sound, listen to the ebb and flow of things
that have come and gone into the ground, that now
  hang suspended,
become the rhythm of one man
in baggy clothes and floppy boots,
and a still urgency of breath,

of neck chords straining,
and releasing, bringing the crinkle
of their faces, the sudden patter
of applause, their dollar bills
released in the empty breeze.

FIGURES,
AN INTERPRETATION
for Giorgio Morandi (1890-1964)

Each of his paintings,
of cups and a bowl,
no more, stark pieces
in blue, gray, and mauve,
in frames made by hands that know
what frames must do:
      hold everything still,
and even as Italy goes to war
the history of light proceeds
over these walls, complacent
and cold in that patient
piece of human understanding
we never speak of, how
      in the implacable
shifting of light
we only witness
what transpires without us.

FOR A GIRL I ONCE KNEW
for Sena

Who made all A's
until chemistry,
(she flunked it one summer,
the first black mark, ever,
on her record), whose dad
had died before she was born.
I'll do better this winter,
she said, and flunked again,
and laughing strangely
failed it again in the spring.
  The campus joke, all A's
and three F's, who finally
took Geology; claimed she'd
best discover the lay of the land.
  I remember her thin, long
limbed, and all those sudden smiles
the day she ran off with a man
not right in his head, and
the quality of her answers
no matter what was asked her.

FOURTEEN REASONS WHY

1. The grandmother hated men, had since she was sixteen and discovered what it was men always wanted.
2. The mother couldn't stand the grandmother, had married, conceived, and divorced in less than a month of misunderstandings.
3. And then they were three.
4. And the mother worked and the grandmother stayed home, and their little girl became a devout Baptist.
5. The men rarely stayed overnight, except on weekends.
6. The mother was once "Queen" of the high school dance.
7. The grandmother was always overweight; dipped snuff and drank on the sly.
8. Their little girl made straight A's, sang and helped conduct the high school choir.
9. The mother married again, two weeks before her daughter's wedding.
10. Their little girl married a bright young English major.
11. Their little girl's first lesbian experience occurred only a few days before her marriage.
12. Their little girl committed suicide two years later. She stepped in front of a car one bright day after a beautiful snowfall in Tennessee.
13. It was her third try that worked.
14. Her note read: *Forgive me. Je suis non-recouverable.*

HAWAII

In the thick sweet smell of burnt sugar
and Plumeria,
under high-ridged shadows of extinct volcanoes,
with cliffs so high the eye loses perspective
and all sense of balance,
      I dream I'm wearing the wrong clothes,
wrinkled, gray corduroy pants, loafers,
a World War II leather jacket.
I can't remember where I am.
      We're sweating, no clothes on, and
nestled in the crook of each other's arms,
almost asleep. The trade winds flow
over our bed lifting away our perspiration.
      The sunlight, the waves, the days
pump regularly, unconcerned as sand,
and I slip into drifting
how out there just over the first horizon,
just below the reach of my hand,
a blue-green ocean washes us
with the smell of the planet's life,
briny and complete,
as if we were never here.

HUGO ON CAMPUS
for Richard Hugo, in Montana

His forehead wrinkled in thought
like a massive scar, he seemed
a monument, and his civilization
asleep, working hard at discovering
what one wanted to work hard at,
and finding it hard work, and
        in a stage whisper, he hisses,
"Isn't she a beauty?" about the coed
he had in bed one night
and couldn't get it up, and
wouldn't you just know it, still
impotent then. . .
        that self-mockery he used to dis-
guise himself from himself, and
making me blush, want to turn away, sane,
not hear the inner workings of his soul,
delicate as maidenhair, like a silky green fern
ripping at your skin, the sudden surprise and pain,
the rush of contact.

LA BELLE DAME SANS MERCI

"Let him twist slowly, slowly in the wind."
J. Erlichman, from the Nixon tapes

"Paradise after burning,
Double-O-Seven," she said,
and left the government.
Ten months later,
like a burst necklace from her neck
the economy starts a strange mad dance;
the old phrases wink out of existence,
no longer operative, and farewell
the old constructions. A riderless
horse amok on main street, nervous,
nameless, and another reality gone wrong.
"Tell me you desire only me," she says,
and touches him once more
with his terrible need.

LOT'S WIFE

She watched him take hold of a rope, tighten it, then swing it, heavy knotted end swishing past her face, bringing it down hard against the animal's flesh, and once again they were moving, single file through the sand, as if chained one to the other. Men are never completely sane, she'd decided that a long time ago, but to have to leave in the middle of the night...her grandmothers had cried out to her not to be abandoned...their faces rising up before her, their skulls hidden beneath the house, hidden from Lot and the followers of Abraham.

Under the stars, caught in the close night air of the desert, she thought not of the city of Zoar as they approached, not even of her daughters' frightened glances, but of what had been abandoned. And a pain had set itself inside her, the keening pain that sings with the ache of stones, of burials and forgotten bones. Lot had never known such pain. How could he? He was a man, was he not, a man who lived his life according to the laws of Abraham. The Lord commands this of us, he had said, and no more, and with no thought that there might be more. Lot had forbidden her the rites of fox and vulture, the ceremony of renewal. He had not even allowed her the skulls of her grandmothers, and so she had hidden them.

Now they were behind her.

Perhaps if she'd given him a son, she thought, he would not have withdrawn. But in spite of her prayers . . . only daughters. Daughters. And then he had turned his face from them all, leaving every morning without a word, his house filled only with the odors of women.

The night was warm, the stars dimming, and her feet dragged in the sand as she watched him drive her daughters before him. They no longer resisted his will. Downcast, they trudged ahead like beasts, incapable of complaining. His daughters. And yet he did not love them; she knew that now. When he brought those two men into the house, she had known that something would go wrong. As if the people would not have grown curious over those two men!

Even in old robes their clean white faces resembled no one who had ever been in the desert. Angels, her husband had said, and perhaps they were; she didn't know. But they had carried strange scepters about their waists. They had come preaching of some strange disaster that would befall their city. But no one in the city had believed. Only her husband had believed, and he had brought them into her home. As if he hadn't known the people would come; as if he were blind to their strangeness and did not notice the foreign accents on their tongues. Angels, he'd said, rushing past her time and again searching for some possible present to offer them. She had never seen him so excited.

And then the people had come. And even now she remembered how through the window she recognized faces of the men of her tribe, like Jubal's, twisted and angry, calling Lot's name. Fists were raised as they pressed forward, and she was afraid. They wanted Lot to hand over these two strangers who had preached the destruction of their city.

And she watched her husband go out to face them. He stood in the doorway with his back to her, blocking the entrance with his body. Lot was a brave man, she knew it, but against so many.... She saw the angels take the small scepters into their hands, whisper strange words to one another, and she fell to her knees, began pleading with them to save her husband. Suddenly she heard Lot's voice rise above all the others', and she could not believe what she heard. He had offered her daughters to the men to do with as they pleased if only they would leave the angels alone. Her daughters, she remembered how they stood together, crying, hugging one another, her precious daughters who had not yet known a man. And in the midst of all else she felt her life had ended, those words still swimming through her being telling her what she had refused to know. She had ceased to care about her life even as the people shoved Lot aside and swarmed through the door.

It was then that the angels caused blindness to come to all who entered, and the people fled in confusion. And her husband began praying aloud to his God, and no one noticed her for she had ceased to care.

They left that evening. She no longer protested. It was no use; now they were truly outcasts. She saw her family stretched out before her single file, stumbling in each other's footsteps. One daughter led the donkey; the other switched it from behind. And Lot followed them, his robe tied tightly about his waist, one end trailing in the dust. She thought of her grandmothers then, the long line of faces that had preceded her into being, and her legs grew numb and weary, and she did not know if she could go on.

The sun was rising as they ascended the last hillside. There were long shadows over the desert. In the distance she could see the city of Zoar. Already her husband and daughters had begun the descent to the gates of the city. She had fallen behind. Lot called out to her, but she did not answer. She had ceased to care for the future. Only her grandmothers sustained her now, a memory of faces which had looked after her, whose remains she had sworn to protect. Abruptly something flashed silver in the sky and she turned around. She wanted then, one last time, to ask her grandmothers a question. It was no use. Everything had changed. It was as if all of her hope remained behind, hidden from her, as if the waters of her life had drained out of her with each step into the dessert.

And as she stood there, a blinding flash washed over her. Suddenly it was impossible to breathe. Her body was caught up in a terrible momentary dance, her clothes falling away, the shadow of the vulture and fox flying from her breasts, her limbs beginning to melt like a body made of wax, her flesh evaporating in waves, until only a dark remnant of ash and shadow remained to outline her form on the sand.

MEDITATION AT POINT REYES

Sir William Occam,
from whom we get the term
Occam's razor, showed us how
to be efficient in our reasoning,
showed us the errors in Saint Thomas Aquinas,
on Aristotle and the Church . . .

Accused of heresy,
he fled on horseback, and
died of the plague in Italy.

We sit on a promontory,
flat surface of sheer black rock;
watch the heavy pound of surf,
the systolic violence in wave and ocean roar.
Higher up, not twenty feet away,
orange-red flowers flutter above the canyon's shore.
Ice plants are magnified in morning light.

In the fourteenth century,
the world shuddered and knew
that Occam was right,
that once again faith and reason
lived in separate camps,
like step sisters who would not
be reconciled.

End of the twentieth century,
computers track the stars, pulsars,
equidistant twin suns in nova,
trapped in a gravity well,
and no one reconciled.

Today, below sheer cliffs
we stand at the western most point,
watch as seals appear, lazily
navigate the brutal ocean wave
and rock of tidal flux.
To see it so easily done takes the breath;
the sea made suddenly serene.

REPORT FROM THOMAS,
TEN YEARS AFTER THE ACCIDENT

1.
In the humid steel-mill air,
dirt of Birmingham, Alabama,
with the taste of beer
in the back of my throat
I watched him start again
how that last time he'd witnessed
a white flash of himself
leaving his body.

2.
The doctor had taken him off
shock therapy, he remembered,
but no one told the nurse,
and she refused to listen.

3.
The only fair result, he whispered,
should end with her murder.

4.
In his dreams, he said,
lately he recalls the vision
of his already dead friend
beneath the car,
and how he'd promised him enough pain
to make a difference, to appease the suffering
of his dying. But it hadn't worked.

5.
He knew why, he said,
and looked me in the eye:
because Occurrence precedes Essence.
But he'd figured it out too late.
Now he was forced to write things down
to keep his reasoning straight.

6.
Everyone has the right to be unique, he's decided,
and that's why he's against reincarnation. It was
a kind of body stealing, or worse, and when he died
he would refuse to come back. He would lie there
with the universe, he said, and rot.

7.
Now that it was too late, he told me, he would like
to go back to school. The first time through his
education didn't take.

8.
Thought that seeing that white flash of one's self
was a sure sign of an inferior personality.

9.
Believed his best liked reason for anything was
Einstein's thirteenth reason for the General Theory
of Relativity, that it was personally satisfying.

10.
Wished Tillich in *The Courage To Be* hadn't fallen back
on technical language to explain the tough parts. After
reading it again, he said, he felt he hadn't understood
something really important to know.

11.
Laughed when the bartender came up to us to ask if
he could just stand there and listen, and would we
like another drink on the house.

12.
Allowed as how he was sorry, really there was nothing
more could be said, and stood up and shook my hand
and returned to a world we'd not spoken of.

RIVERSIDE, ALABAMA
for F. Scott Fitzgerald and Zelda

On the Coosa River, the newly damned
water backs up becalmed and flat
against its banks. Riverside, one jail,
one sheriff, one police car.
Everything else is private property,
bait houses, restaurants, hot spots
of booze and easy women.

Call it what you will, here
with the coke bottles, beer cans,
bass plugs, hope was what was lost.
We go out for a midnight swim; step down
into warm water; know the ooze
of Coosa buried forests
will suck us under.

No, love, the Coosa is nothing
like the Black Warrior. The Warrior
river still runs smoothly seaward
without a stop. Look there,
on the far bank, that house lit up
in the fog. Let's pretend it's yours,
or mine, or ours.

FOR NO REASON

Again, it can't be mended.
You watch me mumbling at the window,
something's lost that we can no longer
get from one another. It happens,
gets broken,
becomes asymmetrical,
and even when we count everything twice,
still, it can't be found.

It slips down in the leaf pile, between us.

In winter air, white slips of paper
blow across the public parking lot.

And now, a sea gull, only one leg,
stands before us on the beach.
He uses the wind as his crutch,
precariously balanced
until he takes the air.

BLACKBIRD

Tonight
there is a blackbird
in the wind, and
I hold myself empty,
move out from the ground,
this blackbird singing,
no sound.

FORT MASON BAR, SAN FRANCISCO
for Gail

She smiles just like before,
but not the same, the same but arriving
from a great distance. A storm's
heavy waves wash the wet dark pier
before us. I nurse a hot brandy.
Steam gathers in my glass.
  It's that she leans into me now
with her smile, somehow centered forward,
a new lever and fulcrum balanced within
her, a new seed centering her universe.
  And even as I see it in her,
I want to say, "Let's go now," but I don't.
Something remains sleeping within me,
a dream I haven't reasoned out,
and so we sit, time holding us suspended
like seals in the sea before us,
unable to go home.

HOLD ME

Out the window the land falls away into gray
bay and boats with furled sails,
a foggy winter's day on the Mendocino Coast.
And then, just flushed from love making,
all red in your plumlike soul,
you ask, still wet and glistening,
if I love you.

Side by side, our bodies still touch.
Kelp beds are bobbing in the surf,
and for a long moment afterwards
I slip back into myself, my historical
self, and remember them,

my first wife in bed
trying a guitar chord
she never quite mastered,

and my second wife,
standing alone in her door,
empty as a silvery abalone shell,

and suddenly I feel the cold
as rain and wind begin to lash
the highway home. Hold me,
I say, watching the waves pound,
and rain drops streaking down
the glass.

OHLONE PARK, BERKELEY

Sunday, the sidewalk breathes in early morning
heat, and suddenly I hear her making love,
so near I can almost feel her
voice rising an octave. I listen, and
something inside me, a school of fish, abruptly changes
directions.
       Stepping into weeds, the sunlight
falls through cedars into an open upstairs
window. Strange black outlines, shadows
move in her voice, move heavily within me,
guiltily listening.
       I press closer into the bushes; imagine
the dark wood of her bed, her
multicolored patchwork quilt, her
once ordered room; stand
in knife-like sunlight, knees
deep in the new green
of blackberry brambles,
       and oh, to be caught up in the will
of a woman, nest in the debris of another's
life, to let go, float freely in the sounds
of her love making, swim in a voice
that knows how what can be broken
can be made whole again.

RUSSIAN RIVER
for Gail

How is it we come to this?
She sits poised at the edge the boat
ribbed in shadows. She speaks of trust.
I talk of what remains.
        Autumn and the glare off the water
lights her red hair. She sits unruffled
and calm while something I wanted
and awkwardly am, begins to spin
inside me.
        I say I am not afraid, but I am.
I have let the boat drift. And as her breath
moves across my neck a strange feeling rushes
through me searching for a place to rest,
and I have been waiting a long time
without knowing it.

SEPTEMBER

In you, tonight, I felt your emptiness,
and yes, I wanted to pour myself
inside it, my hands in your life,
        how it was as we ran the paths
in the park, the dahlias all in bloom,
dusky red, yellow, like flesh
at the center,
        and when we spoke of broken things,
and you said, touch me, hold me,
and I did.

SEX, GENETICS, THE SEA

Like falling backwards in time
toward something I don't comprehend,
if I stand still
if I run forward
that what I see has no name,
slouches away if I look at it,
yet feel in the touch of bones
        in what has gone before,
as if it were a story, like coming home
and finding each other alone while
        a heavy wet log lifts and falls,
        lifts and falls; and with each soughing
the ground shakes, and I need to know more
of the rumpled shapes of our dreaming out loud
together, of the coming storms, the wind
already stirring the curtains,
        of the rising and falling, asymmetrically
falling over your wet-tongued ear,
a seascape of white sky,
a shoreline of succulents,
of ice plants
        and I can see you still,
eyes dazzled in the daylight,
face washed red beside the sluiced
rock slide,
        and the waiting engines of our lives
start forward again, like heavy ships at sea
that can turn only a little at a time,
        creating what we are, the moment
of penetration, of entering another's life,
of losing one's own.

UNDER THE PYRAMID BUILDING

We were
as in a movie;
I kissed her,

ran my fingers under her dress,
touched her with the tip of my tongue,
kissed her

with my fingertips
as a cab driver looked on

the wet pavement, umbrellas and raincoats,
and lovers,

standing there off Broadway,
folded into one another, become
slow moving as statues in the rain,

creatures clumsily awakening,
as if lifting upwards out of stone.

New Work

HAY STACKER

Too small to lift a pitch fork full from
below, I would climb up top and catch each throw,
midair, then guide and drop the load in one motion,
until the wagon would hold no more.
      Then coming out of the dust from the back four acres
I'd be atop the hay, barely able to breathe in the heat,
yet lying back in the wet of my own sweat, almost complete.
      And when we passed beneath the big pear tree
there in the middle of my grandfather's pasture,
I knew how it would be:
I would stick out my hand and
take the pear straight out of the air,
without effort; it would come to me
because it belonged to me.
      I hadn't yet guessed how things could go wrong,
or how it might be to be left alone, or that one
could lose badly and go down at the end
like my mother, shaking and defeated.
      I was, in that moment, simply there
watching my cousins and uncles in the distance, shimmering
in the hot air like mirages in black rubber boots,
with pitch forks in hand,
      and when I took my first dusty bite,
      it was like my first
sinking deep into a woman's body,
almost overwhelming, and I could feel
      the pear's juice sinking into me
as I lay there in the hay-scented air, adrift
and becoming everything around me,
      until suddenly I laughed out loud
      without knowing
what the laughter was about
as it poured out of me
at the top of the tree-high stack
while the future waited,
and I was carried on the harvest to the barn.

POINT PINOLE

We are no longer strangers.
She lies beside me in sunlight,
and already I know her like a memory.
Eyes closed, small veins pulse, eyelids flutter,
and she's freshly fallen into reverie.
Under eucalyptus trees I stare out to sea,
watch as a wooden boat rocks in the waves.
As a tall black fisherman stands,
lifts his catch by the gills.
A big rainbow of a fish,
its tail curls, flesh glimmering.
Across the Bay, the Golden Gate
is washed in pink. But nothing, I think,
is ever as simple as it seems.
Now a giant oil tanker appears,
begins to creep across my view.
Waking, she sits up,
legs straight out like a child, smiles,
burrows in under my arm.
Then, as eucalyptus leaves rustle above us,
suddenly something opens a hole in my chest,
and, to my surprise, I begin to weep.

THE BEARD

Panama City Beach, Florida

After years of being elsewhere, I stand here
looking out my back door at the Gulf of Mexico
as the surf whispers a constant echo,
of blue-green seasons, of sun across wild sea oats,
and I am returning once again to this blinding white sand,
a third set of children at my elbow.
      Only a few hours from Birmingham,
my birth place, I watch as sidewalks steam
from another sudden rain,
and I am back in the South, and on a whim,
I shave my beard of 26 years.
      Then I rediscover my mother in my eyes.
The vulnerability in my face, without its disguise,
rushes over me with bad news. There is a loss of strength,
a confusion of bright blue eyes, double chin,
and sagging white cheeks.
      My failures rush in.
      To my reflection, I try to lie,
      an old story, a long time past,
but it won't hold. My beard was the start
of my way out, my opening statement,
my first refusal to die.

Dana Street, Berkeley

As I climb the stairs behind you,
your freckled shoulders droop beneath your blouse.
With the dishes washed, and the children asleep,
we've turned our attention to tomorrow.
    I place both hands on your hips,
cup cheeks with a squeeze, push,
lift your bottom to help you up the stairs,
enjoy the slippery feel of you
in new white pants.
    Later, in bed, we listen
to the sudden rain in an early winter wind
as it strips the leaves from the trees, brings
threats of breakage into our treetop room
even as it rings with a song
in the long bellowing sounds of our wind chime,
a Woodstock, as it swings in the wind
frantically to and fro, wild tubular cymbals,
loose reverberating pentatonic scales
rising up through the fanning branches
of our much loved, giant redwood tree,
    until suddenly I am afraid
of the coming of this wind, of being swept away,
of losing that whispery touch of your breasts
and your long straight hair
swinging over me like summer.

THE COMPUTER CONSULTANT'S LAST ASSIGNMENT, CHICAGO

Passing by the window,
high up in the Amoco Building,
after a day's work, alone
with cleaning crew and vast
mahogany desks, he stops
as the Chicago night
spreads out down State Street
to the river and beyond.
Yesterday, he was in California.
Tomorrow, New York.
He has been moving fast,
but suddenly, in this moment,
he is quiet, listening,
and a sullen ungovernable impulse
is rising inside him. His fingers
pass through the glass.
What are you doing with your life?
In the dark, small whispers, doubts
swirl about him like the bodies of wild birds,
and suddenly he is weightless,
floats above the silent traffic below.
He can see himself standing alone
through the empty office window.
Take hold, he says,
remember how it was,
step back through the glass
into the room, turn,
and walk away.

YUBA RIVER TIME

Sunlit, what's left behind from 1849,
the slurry running over granite for years
till the Yuba's silt-smoothed stones
gather heat in the summer sun

and the lovers return
for the rocks' offering
of warmth, curves matching her hips,
support for the bones of her back,

and hands take him into
her softest parts
spread open and wet
as the Yuba rushes past

the blackberry vines,
the understory of oaks,
the lovers amongst the rocks,
and the crash and detritus of thought
are washed away.

FISHING
for Gail

Fishing for brim,
a delicate boney fish,
one must go slow,
move with the trees.

A formal activity, yet
it's full of surprises;
we could lie down on the bank,
take off our clothes,
make love in the mud.

Personally, I don't think you'd like
the fishing part, but you'd come anyway,
to watch me, childlike in my thickness,
all wet and matching wits
with the underworld.

But have you ever noticed how color works
with cows in the woods? They blend in,
become tricky creatures suddenly,
try to hook you if they can, explode
out of nowhere, become docile again.

It's how we are with ourselves,
me especially, enthralled in a mood
I can't control, and I don't give in,
easily. But under an empty sky with you
we can try for blue gill, some large
as my hand, and they're leapers, fighters,
dappled as the freckles on your thigh.

CANCER

Safe in our Sierra Nevada
cool mountain breeze, listening to the
hot tub bubbling around us, we lie back
pink in the last of the daylight,
watch a pale green praying mantis
strike a tai-chi pose, become a twig
an uninvolved stick,
a part of a leaf on the deck,
        and then as I'm about to speak
it happens:
the mantis, nature's ninja,
blurs like a film in fast forward,
snags a black bumblebee from flight,
drags it to a sudden stop.
        But then the counter movement of life
swirls before the death bite,
and I watch the diaphanous wings
pull free.
        And as the black bee takes the air,
something inside me sees
a second chance,
the life I have not yet lived.

AN ALABAMA SONG

for Marvin, Stephen, Betty, David, and Cindy

In every direction's a creek,
and mosquitoes. You stand on a promontory
above a lake, a Southern swamp
of drowned trees, and leap
      starkly naked out into space
grab hold of a knot on a rope,
and swing into that joy of recklessness,
a teenager in full flight, of flying
      down the bright, sharp-edged rock face,
leaving everything behind in a rush of fear
before you break free and begin to rise
without a care up into your own weightlessness
      where your body floats in a sky blue day
as you push away from the knotted rope,
and stop for a moment, going nowhere,
a moment when you have let go
      because you know how to begin the fall,
know how to slip into that slow motion roll
of a perfect dive, leave no splash at all, and
enter that soft wet mesh of forgetfulness.

GRACE

Appearing in the sky, a great
gray-blue heron, size of a small child,
drops down out of the wild, lowering
feet, knobby knees, and he swings
in a backwash of wings to a stop
on my rooftop.
　　　　Next to the chimney, on stilts,
he flaps once, then smooths
his near-black feathers
into a tight-fitting coat
all around him.
　　　　I sit and stare. I am not alone.
The oncologist has phoned.
My scans are clean.

THE DANCERS

...with melting wax and loosened strings sunk hapless
Icarus on unfaithful wings... Charles Darwin

On a night north of San Francisco,
the sort of night when you can drive no more,
a night when fog makes your eyes ache
and Highway One abruptly twists into cliffs and seas,
and you feel like you've been underwater too long,
finally, for the sake of the ones who love you,
you turn in at a bar,
        stop the engine, and
in the pool of an incandescent shimmer, cold wind,
light bulb over weathered wooden walkway, and
mixed in with the intermittent music of a live band,
you listen to the weight of the waves as they rush in
headlong, then thump, suddenly, heavily, dropped,
crashing onto the beach bottom somewhere below,
then more distantly, their echo.
        You sit in the car gathering impetus to go inside,
but small flickerings of thoughts keep you with the waves,
mesmerized, not worried about cause and effect, but content
somehow to leave them disparate, uncontrolled, floating in that sea
which is your life, unconnected and alone,
        and then you go in.
        Absolute, the entrance to the bar,
like going into a louder kind of weather
as you move into an assault of sights and sounds,
of the comings and goings of others, of cigarette smoke,
late night drinkers, and suddenly
you take a step backwards inside yourself, alien
as an artifact, witnessing.

        Across the room a man wearing a silk-red scarf
and cowboy boots, stands, takes up a woman by force
and pulls her across the floor.
        But even before they step into the lights
and onto the stage,
        she moves into him, daring him with her dance,
with her eyes, hands clapping like castanets,

and then she takes hold of the hem
and swirls her Spanish skirt,
flaring it wide, holding the eye,
and it is clear she intends playing with him.
    But all the while he is bearing down on her,
angrily flinging one arm to the sky,
and he is stamping down hard as she backs away,
until finally she stops, unable to escape,
waits until he has moved in and blocked all retreat,
his arms stiff as sabers cutting the air around her,
his boot heels counterpoint to the beat.
    But abruptly, before the music can complete,
at the last chord, she ducks down and spins away,
leaving him standing alone, his hands empty of her,
    and the band is taking a break,
and the man and woman are shouting past you now,
each small piece of their fight
entering you like a bad movie,
and the man is missing three front teeth,
and the woman is older than her dance steps
suggest, and she is angrily, unintelligibly,
shoving her fists into his chest, pulling him forward,
the two of them stumbling for the door.

Climate Change: Drought

Recorded by sound technicians at ultra high frequencies:
The cacophony came from a tree besieged by drought
—and from a frenzy of tree-invading beetles.
                                    Science News, 8/30/08

The sounds are ultrasonic,
small implosions,
sounds of a pinon pine dying.

Wood-boring bark beetles
can hear it,
this popping of cells,
liquid transporting cells,
imploding,
this gasping of trees
dying
of moisture loss.

No defensive resin,
no way to pitch them out.

Arriving on the desert wind
the air fills with ultrasonic chirps,
the sound of beetles
the size of match heads
chewing their way in.

WATCHING YOU UNDRESS
for Gail

Tonight, watching you undress was
like falling backwards in time
toward that moment in our past when
    it became clear
nothing would ever be the same.
I had stepped over the line.
Everything would be redefined.
My past life was slipping away, and
what mattered was the new reality that
arrived with the touch of your bones,
    and my new world, my interior life,
remained only a story about to be told,
and so suddenly I needed to know more
about the rumpled shapes
of our dreaming out loud together
    because I knew about the coming storms,
the wind already stirring the curtains, and I could see
the cumulus clouds gathering around you,
because you had stopped and turned,
eyes dazzled by the daylight,
face washed red beside the sluicing rock slide,
because you lay down under me as I entered
into your warmth, your eyes opened wide,
because in that first moment of penetration
before my hands reached into your life, I knew
there was only one path forward, knew it
before our children were born, before
the waterfall of our decisions had swept us into this future,
before that moment, when we were still unknown,
    and I stopped to watch you undress.

THREE SMILES

Nathan's smile, at 14, is like
discovering a camp fire
in the forest
in the dark
just when you thought
you were alone.

Ben's smile, at 16, flashes by,
quick, furtive, shy,
a movement seen
in the corner of your eye,
a note in a bottle lost
on a wind-tossed sea.

Katy's smile, at 12, arrives
teasing and unfinished
but practiced
like an Elizabethan tune,
and in her eyes
there is a flurry of notes,
playful, serious and strong,
breaking over me like a breeze,
whispering and humming her song.

ADVICE

At a coming of age party, for Ben's fourteenth birthday

In the clearing, we adults form a circle.
Ben cross-legged, sits shyly in the center
face aglow in the firelight. Katy Creek gurgles
distantly falling down the mountain granite
to the Yuba. In the dark we take turns telling
of the first kiss, the first fight,
the first embarrassment.
        His older brothers give advice:
        Ezra says don't cheat; I regret every time.
Don't tailgate, never get a tattoo, calculate your risks,
and don't discriminate.
        Caleb says find the people
you respect, be like them.
        Demian explains how it was when he came awake.
Asleep through much of his childhood, he says,
one day he heard his teachers talking,
deciding what to do with him,
and suddenly he thought, wait, I choose
not to let them, and in that instant
he recognized himself, and knew
he had begun,
the first mark on the first page,
the first history that was his own.
        Ben smiles down into the firelight,
reveals nothing, says nothing. Our words,
we all hope, will enter him like leaf mold,
will provide a soil he can grow into,
will allow him, when his spring comes,
to break into blossom.

A Lesson on Dying

for my friend Don Ultan, dying of cancer, and
our conversations about Gerard Manley Hopkins

> At the end
he spread himself thin,
disappeared by degrees,
did not give in,
did not surrender
what was left to him.
> He knew
how it would end,
stayed sane in spite of the pain,
and left us as if suspending a talk,
time to go out for a walk, go
for a visit with a friend,
a poet who's been dead a hundred years,
whose words still echo in our ears, like
leafmeal, soundswell, rain smell,
like wood smoke.

JOIE DE VIVRE

This is salamander weather.
In early morning rain
I stoop down
to little red dragons
marching,
translucent amphibians
who seem to dream
in slow motion
the way home.

As they high step together
over the wet walkway,
I feel light headed,
want to join in
follow an ancient call
toward nowhere
I know how to go.

THREE COWS

Our windshield wipers
pushing away rain,
I see three cows
standing together in an otherwise
empty pasture.

One looks up
as we splash past on our way elsewhere
as if she sees me
across our vast species difference.

And even as we are rushing forward into tomorrow
she stares out at me in silent communion
of what it means to be
at home in the world, today,
in the rain, in that simple connection,
that reasonable proximity
of simply standing
side by side
next to one another.

A NEW KIND OF WEATHER

And so it comes to this:
a gray-white cirrus
trapped in the bowl of the Yuba's
canyon green forest
and I stare down
into an impenetrable soup of air,
waiting.
It's clear enough. I know
the weather is changing.
The wind chimes go almost raucous
in their pentatonic scale,
as doe-brown, newly leafed limbs of oak
bend backwards in a sudden gale,
as three new words dance strangely
in a strained assonance
indolent lymphocytic leukemia.
They go rattling about in my brain
while I stand still
before the coming storm.

THE DROWNING

for Mark Ray, 1962-2006, Head of Keyboard Studies, Manchester College, drowned in the Yuba River, two days after arriving from England, July, 2006.

I step out into evening air, magenta sky,
sun setting over San Juan Ridge, watch
the mountain's shadow cross over the canyon,
carpet of scrub and live oak, hawk riding in the haze,
a thermal breeze carrying him into darkness.

Just this morning another drowning
in the river down below,
another newspaper story,
a victim of a transitory class-5 force.

I listen now for that first moment of night
when everything's gone quiet
when suddenly the river's echoes come alive,
greenish brown water crashing over rocks and leaves,
sounds that rise bumping up through the trees.

But I can't go back inside.
I think of the surprise in the drowner,
his feeling of the weight of water when
it first roiled over him and took him,
and then the next moment when
he hit his first fear of the force
taking him down
under.

Now the moon has arrived, and it's loud with a white
that spills out and covers over the Milky Way,
renders a whole galaxy of solar systems
into background noise,
and abruptly their long light years of travel
are not much more than a blur,
like that beginning that was going under,
and a whole life reduced
to the time left
before he had to take a breath.

For a moment I can almost feel the wind slip
from that life that was racing outward,
witnessed or not,
that sudden knowing that it could not last,
and the gathering speed of his light years spinning
down into a void,
into a place of
no more choice,
of letting go of
what was left to do.

SONATA OF THE PLASTIC CURTAIN

As each hook snaps loose,
its plastic shape exploding toward the ceiling,
you think *maybe this is not happening*
as you feel yourself falling,
your feet slipping out from under, and you
think, *but why now,*
hands flailing, seeing
your naked wife's body
float away in soap suds
and shower spray,
her soft rosy breasts, soapy hands,
large wide brown eyes watching
as you fall backwards from the tub
as from an airplane, the slapping sound
of water striking the disappearing wall
while your hands are busy grasping at nothing
and the sonata of the plastic curtain
reverberates around you as the hooks
in staccato bursts, blast into space,
and you think *maybe this is not real,*
just before you hit the floor,
before the porcelain toilet
slams against your shoulder,
and the music stops,
almost as if someone
turned off the car radio,
leaving you with the traffic,
the humming of an engine,
and someplace else you need to go.

PROMISES TO KEEP

Fog falls over the coastal range.
Heat heaves off the ground.
At the end of the day, in waves,
cold, ocean-gray mists
drift down damp
over my green yard.
     My eyes dim as
I stand at the window
witness the blue shift
from sun shine to shade,
to impenetrable gray.
     At the end, my grandmother was blind.
She shuffled through her house, her fine
gray-brown hair wound tight in a bun.
     I slip into the life of this moment,
lose distance, perspective. My sense of time
disappears. Inside, in the quiet,
I wait for a word I can not say.
     I have gone on drift,
afloat in changing weather. Today
the burdened old apple tree lost a limb.
Outside, a hawk cries out for its mate.

THE BEGINNING SKIER

We ride upwards, side by side on the lift in stark sunlight;
I watch as my daughter's breath coalesces in an icy breeze,
moves ghostlike across tops of green, icicle laden trees.
Skiers far below carve tracks in unadulterated white.

And we laugh as we pass over yet another of the fallen ones.
A snow-boarder writhes about in the new snow pack.
Like a mollusk or a turtle turned on its back,
he struggles, red-faced, to regain his feet, to continue the run.

And I say, teacherly, "That one's going to fall, see...
she's prepared to panic."
Katy replies, simply, "Like me."

But Katy never falls.
She carves her snow plow turns in powder,
never loses control, never stalls.

(Less than an hour before, my sweet Kate, a dreamer,
bunched her bare belly between thumb and forefinger,
and plunged the hypodermic home, insulin,
in the new regimen, in her new life, at age eleven.)

I follow her down the slopes, say, you need
to keep your skis together,
transfer your weight on the turn,
try to pick up speed.

Each trip down the slope she makes her turns neat,
manages as though she knows what is enough,
what can be given up and still keep her feet.

My daughter, my life line, this time is racing
for the bottom, not falling on the icy slopes,
but carving her new line in the snow.
Watching her run, my fear rises
until I realize
I need to let go.
She's going to be fine.
I'm the one coming from behind.

An Early Morning Surprise
for Gail

Prances about in her new pink panties
wears ghost guest of a young girl's smile,
teases me with liquid amber eyes
comes to me with arms held high, in play,
a butterfly mood holding her in sway,

and then self-consciousness sets in
as she stands in her freckles
and pale white skin
quite embarrassed
and a rose red blush
spreads over both her breasts,
the eager one and the recalcitrant one,

and I rush to embrace her fun,
her playful dance and display
I will carry with me all day.

WHAT IT'S LIKE
for Dr. Bill Newsom

The shock of being struck,
blindsided, as they say,
in the middle of an ordinary day
in the middle of a discussion
about wakefulness
with my son and his wife
when the Asian girl runs a red light,
hits us at speed just
as we are making a left turn
for the freeway home,
changes everything.

That's what it's like,
that piece of bad news,
that word coming at me out of nowhere,
the kind doctor's lips still moving,
lymphoma,
the surprise of it
knocking me off course.

I get out of the car,
see the girl is in shock,
want to put my arms around her.
"Where did I come from?" she stammers.
"My name is *Shi Yi Lin*."
There are no easy answers.
She keeps touching her knee.
She's a pretty girl,
with a lovely name.

TO REMEMBER YOU

for Janice

I have to let in all the light
I can bear,
and it's still not enough.

Over the years you have been erasing
all traces of yourself,
pulling everything into the ground
behind you.

Once I believed in your song
the way I believed in maps
and the way home. I was wrong.

You walked off into snow,
left me with the future, and a son
you were never to know.

You live now
only in my most inward life, more
spread out, like pieces of shell at the shore.

LISTENING

(a conversation with myself)

If I told you you have cancer
would you separate out, body of mine,
from me, this self, this mind
that listens and argues for wakefulness
in all things?
      Take that orange flame of a rose
for instance, the one on our doorstep with a perfume
redolent of sex just before orgasm
when merging is the only possibility
before you have to separate.
      I think the mind is the flower of the plant
inside us.
      If I told you you have cancer? You do.
You know it too. You're suffering.
But we are still whole. Here,
let me comfort you. Something happened.
A damaged cell. Unrepaired. Not your fault.
      Someday we will have to separate,
but not now. Today we start to take this walk together,
you and I, a trek across the desert, carrying a back pack
of chemical poisons. They are assaulting you.
      I accept it, you must too.
On a good day, our flower is open.
Listen, I can spread my words on the wind,
for the passing stranger,
for the ones I love the most.
.

AFTER CHEMO

It is what it is,
the facts
cannot be denied.
I am alive,
and I am witness
to the green sheen
of tree moss
in winter rain,
more green
than a lizard's hide,
and soft and furry,
and growing outside
my bedroom window.
Because it's the same
neither more nor less
than me.

LOSING THE LIGHT

It's as if you've been thrown
like a stone
across moments, bouncing
only from surface tension,
knowing you are losing
the here and now,
the world still outside
all around you,
an ordinary day.

RENEWAL

My father's words survive like weeds
around my stepping stones.
"You were always the one..." he spat at me
one Alabama summer,
an angry emptiness, another caesura,
between us, another landmine
I can't disarm.

I was his eldest.
I stepped over him.
I ignored him.

He loved me. He loved me not.

I didn't go to his funeral,
a mistake. As Faulkner said,
"The past is never dead.
It's not even past."

JANUARY

This is no time to be struggling
in sand. Seasons are mere smudges,
erased like ashes on one's forehead.
Dreams fall through these empty nets.
There is no reason to wait
for reasons to become clearer.
The moon will have its way.
Whenever I choose to think, drifting
deeper, that I can give in,
or purchase a peach,
or not see or be
willing to understand,
I come back, and I almost remember
the way geckos and skinks sleep
and wait to lie in the sun
above ground,
and I tell myself   nothing is wasted,
forgive everything.

ABOUT THE AUTHOR

Charles Entrekin was born in 1941 in Birmingham, Alabama. He took his B.A. in English from Birmingham Southern College in 1964. He left Birmingham in 1965 and lived in various states (New York, Tennessee, Alabama, and Montana) while pursuing advanced degrees in philosophy and creative writing.

The Managing Editor of Hip Pocket Press (www.hippocketpress.com), Charles is also the author of four books of poetry from which this collection was drawn: *In This Hour*, (BPW&P, 1990); *Casting for the Cutthroat & Other Poems*, (BPW&P, 1986); *Casting for the Cutthroat*, (Thunder City Press, 1978); *All Pieces of a Legacy*, (BPW&P, 1975).

Charles' novel, *Red Mountain: Birmingham, Alabama, 1965*, was published in May, 2008, by El Leon Literary Arts (www.elleonliteraryarts.org).

For more information: www.charlesentrekin.com, www.hippocketpress.org

www.ingramcontent.com/pod-product-compliance
Lightning Source LLC
Chambersburg PA
CBHW030939090426
42737CB00007B/473